A Visit to a Car Factory

D. M. Rice

TIME
FOR KIDS

Consultant

Timothy Rasinski, Ph.D.
Kent State University

Publishing Credits

Dona Herweck Rice, *Editor-in-Chief*
Robin Erickson, *Production Director*
Lee Aucoin, *Creative Director*
Conni Medina, M.A.Ed., *Editorial Director*
Jamey Acosta, *Editor*
Stephanie Reid, *Photo Editor*
Rachelle Cracchiolo, M.S.Ed., *Publisher*

Image Credits

Cover & p.1 Plus Pix/Photolibrary; p.4 Monkey Business Images/Dreamstime; p.5 top: Robyn Mackenzie/Shutterstock; p.5 bottom: Darren Brode/Shutterstock; p.6 Chad Ehlers/Superstock; p.7 top: Rainer Plendl/Shutterstock; p.7 bottom: MCT/Newscom; p.8 Dmitry Kalinovsky/Shutterstock; p.9 top: Niko Guido/iStockphoto; p.9 bottom: Javier Larrea/Photolibrary; p.10 top: margita/Shutterstock; p.10 bottom: 3DDock/Shutterstock; p.11 MarFot/Shutterstock; p.12 Maros Markovic/Dreamstime; p.13 top: MORVAN/SIPA/Newscom; p.13 bottom left: Gregory Gerber/Shutterstock; p.13 bottom right: Fanfo/Shutterstock; p.14 top: WithGod/Shutterstock; p.14 bottom: Luminis/Shutterstock; p.15 Rainer Plendl/Shutterstock; p.16 Monty Rakusen Cultura/Newscom; p.17 top: Monty Rakusen Cultura/Newscom; p.17 bottom left: Kurhan/Shutterstock; p.17 bottom right: Eduard Stelmakh/Shutterstock; p.18 Vasily Smirnov/Shutterstock; p.19 top: Richard Welter/Shutterstock; p.19 middle: Vereshchagin Dmitry/Shutterstock; p.19 bottom: Huntstock/Getty Images; p.20 background: Laitr Keiows/Shutterstock; p.20 Prodakszyn/Shutterstock; p.21 top: S.Borisov/Shutterstock; p.21 bottom: Monkey Business Images/Shutterstock; p.22 Nigel King/iStockphoto; p.23 top to bottom: Sony Ho/Shutterstock, rodho/Shutterstock, iStockphoto, Bedryk/Shutterstock, Monkey Business Images/Shutterstock; p.24 top to bottom, right to left: Monty Rakusen/Newscom, 3DDock/Shutterstock, Dmitry Kalinovsky/Shutterstock, Laitr Keiows/Shutterstock

Based on writing from *TIME For Kids*.

TIME For Kids and the *TIME For Kids* logo are registered trademarks of TIME Inc. Used under license.

Teacher Created Materials

5301 Oceanus Drive
Huntington Beach, CA 92649-1030
http://www.tcmpub.com
ISBN 978-1-4333-3607-2
© 2012 by Teacher Created Materials, Inc.

Table of Contents

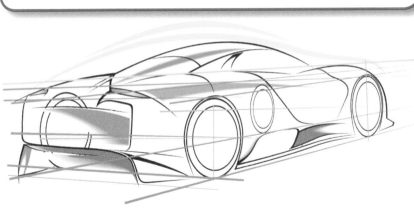

Going to the Factory

One morning my dad came
to wake me up early.

"Surprise!" he said. "You get to come to work with me."

Automobile is another word for *car*.

My dad has the best job ever. He works in an automobile factory. They make cars there.

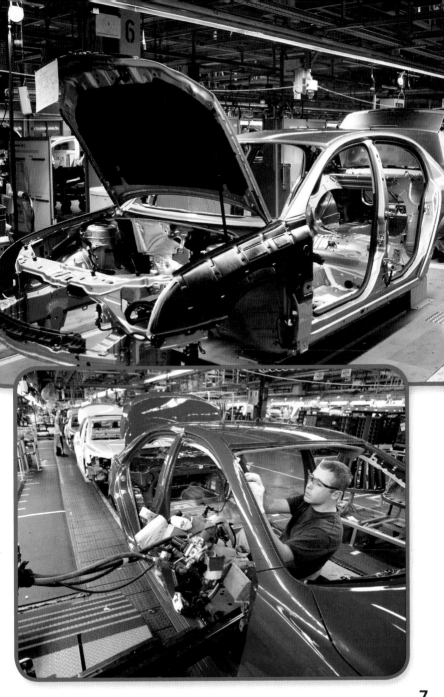

Engineers

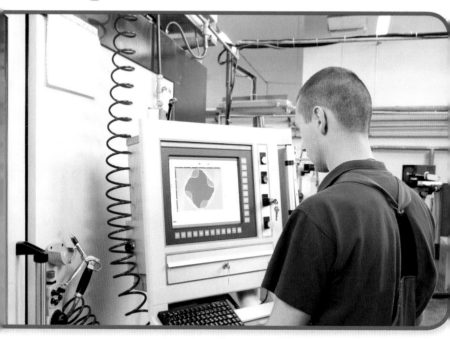

My dad is an **engineer**. That means he helps plan how a car will look and work.

Dad works with other engineers. They work together so the car will be safe and run great.

Dad and his team draw their **plans**. They look like this.

Plans can be drawn using a pen or pencil. Some engineers use a computer to draw their plans.

I want to be an engineer, too. So, I draw my own plans.

Getting the Parts

When the plans are ready, the car can be built. But first, factory workers must make or buy all the parts for the car.

There are hundreds of parts!

A car needs springs, brakes, and a steering wheel. It needs pistons, valves, and more.

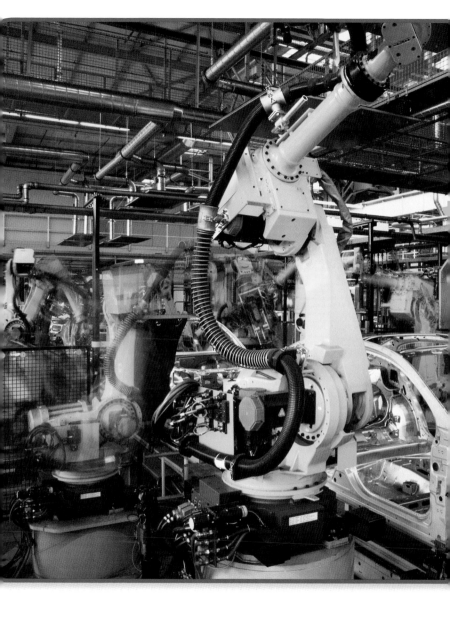

It is not easy to build a car!

Assembly

Once they have the parts, workers can put the car together. This is called **assembly**.

They work in teams. Each team builds a different part of

the car. One team builds the
engine. Another builds the
body. Another is in charge of
the wheels and tires.

There are many teams with many different jobs. All of them are important.

Each team checks its work carefully. They want the

people who drive the car to be safe.

Engineers check the work, too.

Ready for Sale

When the cars are ready, they go to a **shipping yard**. The shipping yard sends them to **dealers**. Sometimes the cars go by boat. Sometimes they go by truck. Then people buy the cars from the dealers.

When I see cars on the road, I feel proud of my dad. He makes good cars for people to enjoy.

When I grow up, I'm going to work at the car factory, too!

How a Car Is Made

Do you know how a car is made?
This chart will show you.

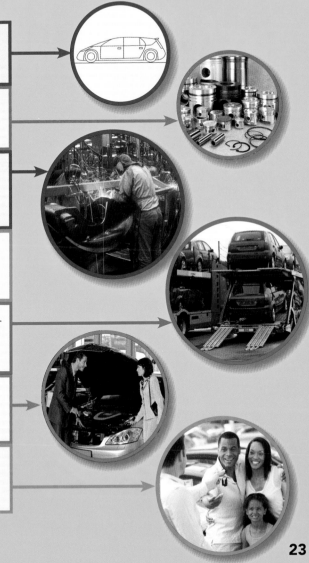

1. Plans are drawn for a new car.

2. Parts are made for the car.

3. The car is put together by teams.

4. The car is checked and tested.

5. The finished car is sent to the shipping yard.

6. The shipping yard sends the car to a dealer.

7. People buy the car from the dealer.

Glossary

assembly

dealer

engineer

plans

shipping yard